A WONDERFUL ADVENTURE

THE LITTLE
Rose Shop

A WONDERFUL ADVENTURE
© 2023 BY THE LITTLE ROSE SHOP. ALL RIGHTS RESERVED.

WRITTEN BY RAQUEL ROSE & EMILY WHITE
ILLUSTRATED BY RAQUEL ROSE

THELITTLEROSESHOP.COM

DEDICATED TO:

AVAMARIE, WADE, AND CLAY
MAY YOUR LIFE WITH CHRIST TRULY BE A
WONDERFUL ADVENTURE

HI THERE, LITTLE ONE!

COME TAKE A RIDE TO SEE.

JUMP IN THE POPEMOBILE

AND SIT NEXT TO ME!

MY NAME IS

ST. JOHN PAUL THE GREAT.

I WANT TO HELP YOU GET TO HEAVEN.

I JUST CAN'T WAIT!

LIFE WITH CHRIST IS

A WONDERFUL ADVENTURE!

OF THIS, YOU CAN BE

QUITE SURE.

SOMETIMES ON THE ROAD

THERE ARE TWISTS AND TURNS.

THESE ARE SIMPLY

OPPORTUNITIES TO LEARN.

WHEN THE JOURNEY GETS

TOUGH OR ROUGH,

TURN TO OUR MOTHER IN HEAVEN,

HER LOVE IS MORE THAN ENOUGH.

I OFFERED MY LIFE TO HER, SAYING

"TOTUS TUUS" WITH LOVE.

LET THIS REMIND YOU,

MARY GUIDES US CLOSER

TO JESUS ABOVE.

THERE IS SO MUCH JOY WITH CHRIST
EACH AND EVERY DAY.

IF YOU EVER GET LOST, BE NOT AFRAID!

LOOK TO OUR GOD IN HEAVEN
HE WILL SHOW YOU THE WAY.

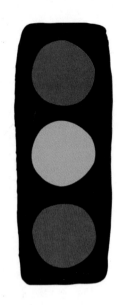

THE ROAD TO HEAVEN IS FILLED WITH

TWISTS AND BENDS, MY FRIEND,

BUT WITH GOD'S GRACE AS OUR LIGHT,

WE'LL REACH A JOYFUL END.

LIFE WITH CHRIST IS A WONDERFUL ADVENTURE
JP II

TOTUS TUUS

BE NOT AFRAID

THERE ARE MANY CHALLENGES

WE WILL FACE,

BUT, YIELD TO THE CROSS OF JESUS.

WITH HIS MERCY,

WE CAN FINISH THE RACE.

IT'S TIME TO TAKE MY POPEMOBILE AND

BE ON MY WAY.

THIS WAS A WONDERFUL WAY TO

SPEND THE DAY.

AS WE JOURNEY THROUGH LIFE,

ON THIS ROAD, SIDE BY SIDE,

I HOPE TO SEE YOU IN HEAVEN,

WHERE ETERNAL LOVE ABIDES.

REMEMBER:

BE THE CHILD GOD HAS MADE YOU TO BE!

THANK YOU FOR TAKING THIS

LITTLE RIDE WITH ME!

MORE ABOUT THE SIGNS

POPE JOHN PAUL II ADDRESSED THE CROWD AT WORLD YOUTH DAY IN DENVER, CO IN 1993:"DO NOT BE AFRAID. DO NOT BE SATISFIED WITH MEDIOCRITY. PUT OUT INTO THE DEEP AND LET DOWN YOUR NETS FOR A CATCH.... I PLEAD WITH YOU--NEVER, EVER GIVE UP ON HOPE, NEVER DOUBT, NEVER TIRE, AND NEVER BECOME DISCOURAGED. BE NOT AFRAID."

DEPICTED ON THE PAPAL COAT OF ARMS. THIS SYMBOL REPRESENTS MARY AT THE FOOT OF JESUS' CROSS.

"TOTUS TUUS" WAS JPII'S MOTTO DURING HIS PONTIFICATE. THE TERM MEANS, "TOTALLY YOURS", REFERRING TO HIS TOTAL CONSECRATION TO MARY. THIS PHRASE ORIGINATES FROM ST. LOUIS DE MONTFORT.

LIFE WITH CHRIST IS A WONDERFUL ADVENTURE
JP II

POPE JOHN PAUL II SAID "LIFE WITH CHRIST IS A WONDERFUL ADVENTURE" DURING HIS HOMILY TO YOUNG PEOPLE IN APRIL OF 1997. "DO NOT BE AFRAID! LIFE WITH CHRIST IS A WONDERFUL ADVENTURE. HE ALONE CAN GIVE FULL MEANING TO LIFE, HE ALONE IS THE CENTRE (SIC) OF HISTORY. LIVE BY HIM! WITH MARY! WITH YOUR SAINTS!"

ABOUT THE AUTHORS

RAQUEL IS A CATHOLIC WIFE, MAMA, AND OWNER OF
THE LITTLE ROSE SHOP. SHE LOVES USING HER CREATIVE GIFTS TO BRING
FAITH INTO EVERYDAY LIFE WITH CATHOLIC INSPIRED TOYS, MUGS,
SHIRTS, AND ANYTHING FOR THE CATHOLIC MAMA TRYING TO RAISE
HER BABIES WITH A LOVE FOR JESUS AND HIS CHURCH.

EMILY IS A CATHOLIC WIFE, MOTHER, EDUCATOR, AND AVID GARDENER.
SHE ENJOYS CHASING HER LITTLES UP THE MOUNTAIN SIDES OF THE
COLORADO ROCKIES, READING OLD FASHIONED BOOKS, GROWING CUT
FLOWERS, AND DRINKING COFFEE WITH COPIOUS AMOUNTS OF CREAM.

BRINGING FAITH INTO EVERYDAY LIFE

THELITTLEROSESHOP.COM

Made in the USA
Las Vegas, NV
24 October 2023

79628672R00021